Relationships Made Easy

How to get along with all kinds of people

by
Sarah Risko Aschenbach

All rights reserved. No part of this book may be reproduced in any form, except for the inclusion of brief quotations in review, without permission in writing from the author.

First Edition: 1998

ISBN 0-615-12672-3

Printed in US by Instantpublisher.com

Table of Contents

Introduction

Do you have trouble with relationships? Do you think it's all your fault? Have you tried everything you can think of to get through to the people in your life?

Maybe it's your mother, your boss, an annoying co-worker or your most significant other, but if you are like most people, it's very rare when all your relationships are in tip-top shape.

Don't give up. There *is* something you can do. This little book lets you in on some secret knowledge about human behavior, practical know-how you can use right away to understand the people in your life: how they look at life, how they see you, what's important to them and how to communicate with them in a way they find comfortable.

Many years ago, when I was lamenting about chronic problems in a long-standing relationship, a friend commented, "It seems to me that if you have been trying the same thing over and over and it isn't working, it's time to try something different." Such simple words, but what a revelation! It was true. I thought I knew exactly what was wrong and the only way to fix it, so I just kept doing the same thing over and over. All my effort was focused on either beating myself up for being who I was or trying to change the other person. Instead, I needed to change the way I was looking at the problem; I needed to see it in a new way so that I could stop repeating the same pattern over and over. That was the first time I realized that my own point of view was keeping me stuck and unhappy.

This book will introduce you to the nine personality types of the Enneagram (ANY-a-gram). I have described each of them at home and at work, how they react to stress, and what they are like at their best. At the end of each type description are a few tips for creating rapport and avoiding or defusing relationship conflicts. There is a section on how each type might respond to a common workplace issue, and another section providing guidance on how each type can reach its highest potential.

The names given to the types provide a brief way of referring to a whole set of characteristics. The numbers assigned to the types do not signify value; that is, a Nine is not more or less advanced than a One. Last, although the images sometimes depict a female and sometimes a male, there are both males and females of every type.

I have deliberately made this book a concise and easy reference that is small enough to carry wherever you go. Its purpose is simple—to give you some profound information on human interaction in an easily accessible form. I guarantee it will improve in your personal and professional relationships.

It all begins with you. There is nothing you can do to change another person. However, you can change yourself. You can learn to look at the world—and your problems—in a new way.

If the same old thing isn't working, for heaven's sake try something different!

How to Use This Book

Relationships can be much easier than they are. How?

- First, read this book and identify your own type. Acknowledging how you may come across to others when you are under stress is the first step.

- Second, try to identify the people you are dealing with. The best way to do this is to ask them to look through this book and identify themselves. Discuss what you have discovered about yourselves and how the differences in your personality types are affecting your communication.

- Third, choose just one tip for getting along with each other. Commit to put the suggestion into practice for a specific time (make it short in the beginning; perhaps an evening or the rest of the day). Give each other positive feedback when the opportunity arises. For example, "I liked it when you smiled and said hello as soon as you came in the house." Or, "I really appreciated it when you gave me time to figure out what I wanted to say."

- Last, a caution: never assume that you are the best judge of someone else's personality type. Do not tell others what type you think they are. Do not beat them over the head with this information or tell them how you think they need to change. Instead, give them this book and ask them to try and find themselves in it. The discovery of one's type must unfold on its own from inner awareness. Inner awareness is what brings about lasting change.

As an aid, I highly recommend that you take a comprehensive personality test, the Riso-Hudson Enneagram Type Indicator (RHETI), as a way to make certain that you and the people in your life have accurately identified your personality types.

If it is not possible to share this process with the other person, try out tips that may apply and see what happens. Remember, doing just one thing differently may be enough to give you an entirely different outlook on your relationship.

Here's my first tip: put a copy of this book on your desk or coffee table. Who knows, maybe someone will recognize *you* in these pages...and how *you* like to be treated!

Type One

The Reformer

How to Recognize a One

At work, Ones are the people with the neat desks and sharpened pencils. No messy piles of papers for them. In fact, Ones will fret over a small pile of papers that collects in the course of a busy morning and beat themselves up for the mess. They are punctual, and many Ones pride themselves on getting to work half an hour early. They are organized, efficient and meticulous about the quality and quantity of their work. Ones expect themselves to uphold the highest standards and consider it an obligation to be reasonable, fair and truthful. They speak in terms of "shoulds" and "should nots."

Average Ones are so determined to improve themselves and everything around them that they can begin to irritate their bosses and co-workers. Most people don't care that much about a typo in a memo that went out to three people, but Ones feel obligated to point it out anyway. And they can't understand why anyone would be offended by "The Truth."

At home, Ones are equally principled and orderly. Their homes must be neat, a place for everything and everything in its place, and they can't relax until everything is perfect, which means they can never relax. They have tremendous self-discipline when it comes to living up to their ideals, whatever they may be, and they try to do everything as it "should" be done. Ones consider it an obligation to set a good example for their friends and loved ones, and are disappointed in themselves when they display ordinary human weaknesses.

Ones under Stress

Under stress, Ones become increasingly critical of themselves, others and the environment. They feel everything and everyone needs shaping up, and they are impatient and angry with others who seem too casual about doing what is right. When others dismiss or ignore their concerns and criticisms, Ones only try harder to justify themselves and convince others that they are wrong.

Ones at their Best

Liberated Ones realize that it is not up to them to judge others and that, in fact, there is not just one right way to approach life. As they relax and accept their own needs and feelings, they develop the wisdom to be tolerant of others' needs and feelings. When Ones gain true objectivity, they realize they are not in a position to preach to others. By hearing others out impartially and giving them the room to find their own truths, Ones truly achieve their objective of teaching others by their example.

Tips for Getting Along with Ones

- Get your facts straight and present what you have to say logically and clearly.

- Acknowledge how hard Ones try to do a good job and be a good person.

- If you can see that Ones do a task well and want to avoid their criticism, ask them to teach you.

- Keep your word. Be truthful, but sensitive to their feelings. Ones will respect you for it.

Type Two

The Helper

How to Recognize a Two

Twos have wonderful people skills. At work, they are the ones who always remember to ask how *you* are and are quick to offer help or a sympathetic pat on the back if they sense you are overwhelmed. They bring in the donuts and pass around candy and never forget a birthday. They go and get tea or coffee for harried co-workers and offer to brew a fresh pot when it is empty. When others don't do the same, Twos put up signs in the coffee area saying, "Your mother doesn't work here, so please be thoughtful."

Average Twos may run into trouble with the boss or less outgoing co-workers because they seem too personal or spend too much time socializing. They may gossip, convincing themselves that they are only trying to help by making everyone aware of a co-worker's problem.

At home, Twos keep busy doing helpful things for family and friends. They have many, many "best friends." They enjoy engaging others heart-to-heart, and they like to talk about relationships and feelings. Twos are affectionate and demonstrative, and they expect others to show their love in the same way. They spread themselves thin trying to "be there" for others. This may mean being available for phone calls in the middle of the night, taking soup and presents to people who are sick or stressed-out, organizing birthday parties, running errands, helping people move, writing resumes for friends and relatives, giving advice and making sure everyone is bundled up against the cold and has taken plenty of vitamins.

Twos under Stress

Under stress, Twos complain about how much they do and how little it is appreciated. They can become quite bossy and manipulative, though they don't want to see this about themselves. They may make others feel guilty: "Here, you take the good chair. I'll take the broken one. No, no, I insist." Some Twos become hypochondriacs, expressing stress through vague complaints or real illness.

Twos at their Best

At their best, very healthy Twos realize that unconditional love for themselves and others can only come from a higher source or a deep inner state, and they lose the need to prove they are lovable. They love themselves and give themselves what they need, which frees them to give to others in a balanced way, without expecting anything in return.

Tips for Getting Along with Twos

- Be friendly. Greet Twos with a smile and a pleasant word, no matter how busy you are.

- Remember what's going on in their life and show your genuine interest or concern.

- Don't let Twos do more for you than you're willing to do for them.

- Offer to lend a hand before they ask, or send a card when they don't expect it.

Type Three

The Achiever

How to Recognize a Three

At work, Threes are goal-oriented, efficient and effective. They take their work seriously and do their best, whether they are running a company or jogging through the park, because whatever they are doing is always preparation for the next highest step. They have an instinctive feel for how to make a good impression wherever they are, and they rapidly advance to the most influential positions. They dress for success and speak with self-assurance and energy about setting and achieving goals.

Because they put their feelings aside to "do what has to be done," others sometimes see them as cold or unfeeling. Average Threes are also very competitive, which can either offend others or motivate them to strive harder. They can seem too smooth and may try to hide their mistakes.

At home, Threes strive just as hard to make their personal life a success. They have goals for their marriage, their home and their children. Threes want recognition for the "good life" they make possible through their efforts. Average Threes, however, can become so caught up in their achievements that they neglect their families. Making a good impression by having the best house, clothes, furnishings, friends, activities and social standing can begin to get in the way of true personal achievement and meaningful self-development.

Threes under Stress

Under stress, Threes compete harder, even with friends and family. They have to "be the best," get the most attention, be the "favorite." To keep themselves from giving in to a nagging fear that they will fail, they brag about their accomplishments. They also can become jealous and do little things to make others look less successful. Sometimes under stress, Threes drive themselves so hard that they go numb, working on autopilot until they collapse.

Threes at their Best

At their best, very healthy Threes are the role models we all look up to. They realize that their real value is not something they can find in others' eyes. Valuing themselves truly for their inner worth frees them to reveal themselves to others, warts and all. Through their own real self-development, they inspire others to do the same.

Tips for Getting Along with Threes

- Give Threes lots of attention and let them know you value them, but don't push for intimacy.

- When you have something to say, get to the point quickly.

- Because professionalism and appearances are so important to them, avoid criticizing them or making a "scene" in front of others.

- Present problems as challenges.

Type Four

The Individualist

How to Recognize a Four

At work, Fours may seem unapproachable, but once you draw them out, they are warm and sensitive. Small talk doesn't interest them much; they prefer to communicate on a deeply personal level. They gravitate to work that engages their creativity. Even in a job they consider "mundane," they find ways to express themselves—color coding their to-do lists, decorating their file folders or trying out different accents while serving customers. They dress to suit their moods and always do something to stand out from the crowd, like wearing an offbeat vest with the standard business attire.

Average Fours are afraid that something is wrong with them and that everyone but them can see it. They can look chronically dissatisfied, no matter what they are doing. They are also highly sensitive to even the barest hint of criticism, which can be especially difficult in a work situation.

Fours create a pleasing and distinctive atmosphere at home. Their surroundings evolve around them as they collect unusual pieces of furniture and art, interesting pillows, the odd assortment of pottery. They prefer small, intimate gatherings and are uncomfortable with people they don't know. Unless they are involved in a new intimate relationship, they like to spend much of their free time alone, reading, puttering around the house, listening to music, starting various projects and fantasizing about love, personal recognition and a time when they will be able to live a totally free and creative life. These preoccupations, of course, interfere with their ability to maintain successful relationships and realize their dreams.

Fours under Stress

Under stress, Fours begin to feel that no one understands or appreciates them for their unique gifts. They become moody and hypersensitive, hoping that others will recognize how unhappy and misunderstood they are. As stress increases, they demand the right to do only what they want to do when they want to do it. When this attempt is met with resistance, Fours are prone to emotional outbursts, shame and depression.

Fours at their Best

At their best, very healthy Fours let go of the belief that something is wrong with them.

They realize that all people, including themselves, are originals, one-of-a-kind. They are emotionally strong, intuitive and sometimes inspired, and they touch others through their self-revelation.

Tips for Getting Along with Fours

- Try not to be put off if Fours seem aloof. They are probably wondering whether you like them.

- Provide them with supportive social opportunities to build confidence.

- Understand that they react emotionally when dealing with conflict and don't criticize them for showing their feelings.

- Help them establish a personal connection to the task at hand.

Type Five

The Investigator

How to Recognize a Five

Fives live in the world of ideas. At work, they gravitate to information-oriented jobs: computers, engineering, research, academia, technical consulting. Fives can seem a bit odd at first. Some Fives are quiet and stay to themselves, while others keep on the lookout for people who are interested in their ideas or their area of expertise. They like to solve problems, but they will quickly disappear or put you off if your problem bores them. Their work area may seem unbearably messy to you, but they know how to find anything that matters to them.

Average Fives can get quite prickly if you interrupt them or make even small demands on their time. They also tend to think they are much smarter than everyone else, including the people they report to, which understandably can lead to problems.

At home, Fives like to spend a lot of time reading, listening to informative programs, surfing the Net and talking about their latest theories. They are a fountain of information, both practical and obscure. Most Fives collect piles of papers and mountains of books, and it irritates them if anyone presses them to "clean up" or, heaven forbid, to throw away some of it. They want lots of space in their relationships so they can pursue their interests with minimum interference, and they are therefore inclined to give their partners plenty of space. They tend to analyze their own and others' feelings and really benefit when someone can gently help them to stay with and express their feelings.

Fives under Stress

Under stress, Fives slow down, putting off what needs to be done until they feel prepared to tackle it. Preparation means gathering more information, drawing up plans, making lists and so forth. The more they delay, the more critical their situation becomes, which makes them prickly and high-strung and even more pressed for time. Fives may become so preoccupied that they stay up too late, eat haphazardly and neglect even basic hygiene.

Fives at their Best

At their best, very healthy Fives realize that they can engage with life fully *now*. They understand that the outside world is not something they must defend against or prepare themselves to meet. They move confidently into action, focusing their keen minds and communicating their insights clearly. They are the visionaries who show us how to look at the world in a brand new way.

Tips for Getting Along with Fives

- Be prepared when you approach them and say what you have to say logically and clearly.

- Don't "charge" Fives. Give them time to assimilate new information and switch gears.

- Don't cling. Pursue your own interests and give them a reasonable amount of time and space.

- To get closer, show genuine interest in one of their areas of expertise.

Type Six

The Loyalist

How to Recognize a Six

Sixes take their responsibilities seriously and are very loyal and dependable workers. They believe in pulling their own weight and they encourage everyone to pitch in and work together. "Many hands make light work" could be their motto. They like rules. They are the people most likely to put up signs in the workplace kitchen area saying, "When you empty the coffeepot, make a fresh pot." Sixes tend to knock themselves out trying to do everything that's expected of them. They check in with the boss to make sure they are on the right track and become fearful if they don't get the reassurance they need.

Average Sixes keep taking on more work from the boss while complaining about it to others. They notice who does and who does not follow the rules. They also have a tendency toward *in* group/*out* group thinking, which can undermine the very team spirit they crave.

At home, Sixes strive hard to maintain a secure and dependable family space. For the most part they do their chores without being reminded, but if they feel others are taking advantage of their good nature, they may balk or engage in passive-aggressive maneuvers. When reasonably healthy, they are loyal partners, committed parents and responsible and active members of their community. However, they need lots of approval and they need to be convinced over and over that there is something or someone they can rely on. Sixes tend to anticipate problems and become quite fearful over matters that seem trivial to others.

Sixes under Stress

Under stress, Sixes begin to vacillate between caving in and taking a tough stand. If they feel torn between, for example, the demands of their job and their family obligations, they may first try to make everyone happy then suddenly turn on one or both of the "authorities" that they feel are trying to tear them apart. Such an outburst, however, is likely to make them even more anxious and eager to please as they try to regain the security they fear they have lost.

Sixes at their Best

At their best, very healthy Sixes realize that they can rely on themselves to handle whatever life brings. Instead of worrying about whether they belong and seeking reassurance, they

23

become a dependable source of support to others. Secure in themselves, they widen their circle and provide a positive rallying point. They are capable of creating and maintaining organizational structures that are fair and clearly defined.

Tips for Getting Along with Sixes

- Let Sixes know where you stand and what you expect of them.

- Talk about the ways in which you are similar.

- Give them lots of reassurance, verbal and non-verbal, and in a conflict, let them know you will stick with them and work it through.

- In a work situation, be as clear and consistent as possible about the rules, and be fair.

Type Seven

The Enthusiast

How to Recognize a Seven

Sevens are the people who keep the energy high and the mood upbeat in the workplace. They are fun-loving, quick with a joke and would prefer to get along with everyone although it doesn't always work out that way. They like to keep things moving along at a quick pace and they crave variety. They do best in jobs that call for multitasking and provide options for how they organize their day.

Average Sevens tend to be talkative and somewhat boisterous, and they are easily bored. They do everything fast and can be impatient with people whom they see as plodding and inefficient. Quieter co-workers may find them irritating—too much of a good thing—but that can be helped by putting some physical distance between their work areas. Sevens may run into problems with the boss because they like to challenge authority.

Sevens are the life of the home and the life of the party. They love sharing their interests with others. They are multitalented, the kind of people who can play a musical instrument, fix the computer and build a fence with equal ease. They collect people and things and experiences, and they are always willing to try something new—and drag everyone else along with them. Average Sevens think more is almost always better. They speak in superlatives. Everything is "wonderful," "terrific," "awesome." They also make big promises that, too often, they forget to fulfill. When reminded, they apologize profusely and expect to be forgiven. Negativity in any form really turns them off.

Sevens under Stress

Under stress, Sevens try to run away from their anxiety. Their activity level increases as they try to keep themselves "pumped up," and they are prone to excesses of all kinds. They fear that they will never get what they need to feel satisfied, and this fear makes them pushy and demanding. When they see that this is alienating others and causing them even more pain, they up their efforts to escape or to deaden their anxiety.

Sevens at their Best

At their best, very healthy Sevens realize that real fulfillment can never be found outside themselves. Instead of squandering their abundant energy, they channel it into productive action that enables them to realize their highest dreams. They learn to savor their experiences, and this brings them the true satisfaction they have always longed for.

Tips for Getting Along with Sevens

- Don't be critical or pessimistic when you approach Sevens.

- Be clear and firm about what you will and will not accept, and don't make exceptions.

- When possible, give them options to choose from rather than commands.

- Help them face their anxieties in a gentle and supportive way. Don't push or they'll run away.

Type Eight

The Challenger

How to Recognize an Eight

Eights like to be in charge. Everywhere. At work, if they are not the boss, some people will think they are, and the real boss had better be one smart cookie or things will get out of hand. Eights don't ask, they tell. They are decisive: they know what results they want and they go straight at it. They exude self-confidence. They challenge people and keep everyone on their toes. If Eights feel they don't have all the resources they need to achieve their objectives, they go out and get them. They are not afraid to take risks.

Average Eights run into trouble by being too abrasive and by charging ahead without testing the waters. Bosses of other types may get rid of them rather than engage them in battle, and co-workers may resent their blunt, no-nonsense manner.

At home, Eights rule the roost. Their word is law. No means No. No discussion is necessary. They provide for their families according to their role in the family circle, and they are fiercely protective. Control is the operative word, and they are determined to maintain control at all times. When relatively healthy, they control the space, the resources and the scheduling of events quietly but firmly—or they magnanimously bestow parts of that responsibility on someone else. As uncompromising as this scenario undoubtedly is, Eights can be pillars of strength to their loved ones, and you can depend on them to tell it like it is.

Eights under Stress

Under stress, Eights are even more controlling if they sense that others do not respect them or appreciate their strengths. They demand absolute loyalty and their control is heavy-handed. They boast and make big promises to increase their sense of importance, and they are quick to believe that others are not backing them up as they should. Because they will not compromise, they are increasingly difficult to be around. "It's my way or the highway!"

Eights at Their Best

At their best, very healthy Eights realize that being in control of things outside themselves is an illusion. They discover that they have all the resources they need inside and lose the need to convince themselves or others of their strength. They open their hearts to others, championing the underdog and inspiring and empowering others.

Tips for Getting Along with Eights

- When you approach, talk straight; be direct and honest.

- Be as independent as possible.

- In a conflict, look them in the eye and stay firm without being combative.

- Eights really enjoy a good fight. If you don't, it's better to keep your distance and save your strength for when it really matters.

Type Nine

The Peacemaker

How to Recognize a Nine

At work, Nines are the people who are most agreeable and non-threatening. Some Nines are fairly quiet, but they are pleasant when approached and are quick to respond if you ask for help. Others are a bit more outgoing and humorous. Nines speak in a calm, easygoing manner and do their best to promote harmony and understanding in a group. "Oh, I don't think she meant anything by that," they might reassure a co-worker. Any disruption in the peaceful flow of life offends them, and they withdraw.

Average Nines go along with whatever anyone proposes, at least outwardly. They can get in trouble with the boss when their accommodating nature leads them to say yes to requests they should refuse and thus get distracted from their own work. Nines also go on autopilot and can spend far longer than necessary on a task.

At home, Nines like a calm atmosphere and discourage or retreat from open displays of conflict. They like their routines, their little comforts and ample time to themselves. They like to go with their own flow, which is like a pleasantly warm current of water that buoys them up and carries them along effortlessly. In social settings, they tend to disengage, as if they are not paying attention, but they feel disregarded if others do not include them in the conversation.

Nines under Stress

Under stress, Nines prefer to retreat. Disengaging from the struggle gives them a stoic quality, which seems to serve them well in a crisis but may also keep them from taking decisive action before a situation escalates. If their first line of defense does not work, they may become unresponsive, and then increasingly stubborn. They turn their backs on people, literally, and give others the silent treatment. Their constant suppression of their natural instincts and feelings builds up over time, and some Nines explode occasionally while others simply "shut down."

Nines at Their Best

At their best, very healthy Nines realize that their participation in the world is important and meaningful. They recognize that friction is necessary for growth, and they can accept the messiness of life and be patient with others' turbulence. Fully aware of the world around them and the life force within, they heal others with their steady and peaceful presence.

Tips for Getting Along with Nines

- Approach Nines calmly and gently and let them know you share their desire for harmony.

- Give them your full attention.

- If you can see that they are holding in their feelings, gently bring it to their awareness, without judging them.

- In a conversation, give Nines the time they need to express themselves.

A Workplace Scenario

Yours is a small company, and you have always given your employees flex time. Recently, you have decided that at least one person must be in by eight a.m. You decide to put the staff members on weekly rotation, excluding yourself and the two supervisors. You sense some resistance. Look for these spoken and unspoken messages. You certainly don't have to accommodate them, but it might be useful to know what's behind the resistance.

Ones

"This had better be fair or I won't stand for it."

"It's not right for some people to be excluded from the rotation."

"Why? What's the logic behind this?"

Twos

"I feel so bad for Mary. She's really stressed out now and she doesn't need the pressure of having to get here so early, too. I know! I'll offer to sub for her when she can't make it. Or maybe I'll talk to the boss about it and ask her to take Mary out of the rotation."

"After all I've done for the boss, and she just lumps me in with everybody else. I really feel unappreciated, and I'm hurt that she didn't at least tell me she was sorry."

Threes

"In three months I'll be a supervisor and this won't apply to me anymore. Till then, I'll go the extra mile and more."

"What's the goal?"

"How can I benefit from this?"

Fours

"You don't seem to understand how this affects me and how I feel about it!"

"I can't come in early on Fridays because I have a late-night poetry reading every Thursday."

"I'm not a drone who can work according to some rigid timetable. I was meant for better things than punching some time clock."

Fives

"Why? What's the rationale behind this?"

"This is really going to be draining."

"I'll do it when I have the stamina, but I don't function at my best when I'm pushed."

Sixes

"Is this written down anywhere so I can make sure I know what I'm supposed to do?"

"What happens if somebody forgets to come in early?"

"I don't see why some people get special treatment."

Sevens

"I hope she's not trying to turn this place into a jail. I need my elbow room."

"This is a drag—I'll come in somewhere around that time and see if anyone says anything when I'm late."

"It's no big deal, and I'm sure I can get around it if I have to."

Eights

"Are you tough enough to back this up?"

"If I was in charge—and I will be someday—everybody would be in here at eight on the dot!"

"I make my own rules. Let the chips fall where they may."

Nines

"I hope this all goes smoothly."

"I don't like this unfairness, but no point in saying anything."

"You've got to go along to get along."

How to Achieve Your Highest Potential

Ones

- Schedule regular time to relax and play and enjoy the healthy pleasures of life.

- When you feel others have wronged you or violated principles that you hold dear, try to give them the benefit of the doubt. Maybe they see it differently or are trying to make amends in their own way.

- Resist the temptation to point out others' mistakes or shortcomings, and when you forget, notice the effect you have on others.

- Be kind to yourself. Everyone is allowed to make a mistake from time to time.

Twos

- Be your own best friend. Look to see what you need and what you can give yourself, and take the time to do it.

- Turn off your phone ringer and turn on your answering machine with the volume off.

- Don't accept invitations or do favors until you have given yourself time to think it over. Practice saying, "Let me check my schedule and I'll get back to you."

- Examine your motives and your own needs before you give a gift or offer your time.

Threes

- Be a real friend to others. Encourage and inspire them to achieve their personal best.

- Be aware of your tendency to put your emotional life on hold and schedule regular time to acknowledge and process your feelings.

- When others have contributed to your success in any way, thank them and give them the credit they deserve.

- Invest in meaningful personal growth work, work that inspires you to explore your inner world.

Fours

- Use your creativity to organize your life and motivate yourself.

- Do at least one constructive thing a day that you don't "feel like" doing, just to exercise the "muscle" of your will.

- When you're too blue to get out of bed, call a friend or write in your journal, then walk to the mailbox or clean the sink.

- Consider this: you don't have to suffer to be creative and being happy will not make you boring.

Fives

- Get in touch with your body. Take up a sport or physical activity that coordinates your body and your mind.

- Do therapy or emotional release work to help you feel your feelings.

- Pick one small project you've been keeping on hold, break it up into small, manageable tasks and commit at least one hour a week until it is completed.

- Set aside some time to be available to your loved ones on a regular basis. Open your heart to them and graciously receive what they have to offer.

Sixes

- If you are obsessing over a worst-case scenario, call to mind a time when you were just as afraid but everything turned out all right.

- Notice when you are getting caught up in your mind and bring yourself back into your body. Feel your arms and legs. Breathe.

- If you feel uncomfortable about something you have been asked to do, don't do it.

- Anyone worthy of your loyalty will be able to respect your limits.

Sevens

- Reflect on your present excesses and ask yourself how much true satisfaction they have given you.

- Examine your dreams and set realistic goals. Do some small thing every day, no matter how mundane it seems, to bring you one step closer to their realization.

- Harmonious relationships are essential to a happy life. Cultivate more awareness of the people around you and how you may be "rubbing their fur the wrong way."

- Give yourself regular quiet time, alone.

Eights

- Relax and let yourself be human. Others will respect you more if you can let your guard down a little from time to time.

- Notice how your tendency to be abrasive hurts others, and try to curb it a little.

- It's not true that everyone will take advantage of you if you let them. Look around and notice the people you *can* trust.

- Use your strength and your resources to empower others. Through giving, you will receive far more than you can take by force.

Nines

- Become aware that you do have preferences and practice expressing them, beginning with small things.

- Realize that others can't read your mind. You can't expect them to be considerate if they don't know what you want.

- Engage in healthy physical activity every day or do ongoing body work.

- Get the help you need to get in contact with your emotions through therapy or other personal growth work.

Overheard on the Street (and Elsewhere)

Ones

"But why should he be mad? It's the truth!"

"If there's anything I can't stand, it's someone who is too cowardly to stand up for what he believes in."

"There's absolutely no other way of looking at it. I know I'm right."

Twos

"I need a hug."

"My problem is, I have too many friends and I don't have time for them all."

"It's a shame his friends and family don't help him change his behavior."

Threes

"I'm a very important person. I don't have time to talk to you right now."

"It's not a problem. It's a challenge. And I like challenges."

"Let's just cut to the chase and get this project underway."

Fours

"You just don't understand!"

"There's something about funerals. They seem to bring out the best in people. Do you know what I mean?"

"It's hard for me to do things if I'm not in the mood."

Fives

"Listen and maybe you'll learn something."

"Would you like me to explain the difference between analog and digital? It's fascinating."

"I'll need a lot more information before I can make a decision like that."

Sixes

"I was sick and tired of asking you before making any decisions, so I told them to go ahead and move the copier into your office."

"We're not allowed to do that."

"She's leaving early. Maybe she doesn't like me."

Sevens

"Let's hurry up and go so we can hurry up and get back."

"All right, you worm-faced weasels, you pack of burbling bombasts, turn your time sheets in now or I will beat you with this leftover noodle!"

"Make people laugh and you get your way."

Eights

"I hate it when people ask me what they should do. I don't have any respect for people who don't know what they want."

"Honey, I'm not pushing you around. Believe me, if I pushed, you'd fall over."

"If I don't like something, I'll tell you right to your face."

Nines

"Yes, she left me after 11 years. Oh, well, that's how it goes. But don't worry about me. I'm okay."

"If you don't know what you've done to upset me, I'm certainly not going to tell you."

"Oh, all right. I don't care one way or the other."

About the Author

Sarah Aschenbach is a personal coach, professional speaker and organizational healer with over fifteen years' experience in working with individuals and groups, both privately and in a corporate setting. She has been certified to teach the Enneagram—the dynamic personality typology being embraced internationally as today's most in-depth and revolutionary tool for understanding human behavior and interpersonal relationships—by Don Richard Riso and Russ Hudson, best-selling Enneagram authors. Founder of Inspired Solutions℠ and developer of EnneaDrama℠, Ms. Aschenbach conducts experiential workshops for individuals and organizations.

Acknowledgments

I am deeply indebted to the work of Don Richard Riso and Russ Hudson of the Enneagram Institute. Their comprehensive training programs and the depth and thoroughness of their approach to the Enneagram have made a deep impression on my own work. I want to thank them and acknowledge Don Riso, particularly, for the Levels of Development, without which I do not believe the Enneagram can be effectively taught.

I encourage all readers to further their exploration with the following books and materials:

Riso, Don Richard, and Hudson, Russ,
Discovering Your Personality Type,
Revised and Expanded, Houghton
Mifflin, 2003.

Riso, Don Richard, with Hudson, Russ,
Understanding the Enneagram, Revised
Edition, Houghton Mifflin, 2000.

Riso, Don Richard, and Hudson, Russ, *The
Wisdom of the Enneagram*, Bantam Books,
1999.

Riso, Don Richard, with Hudson, Russ,
Personality Types, Houghton Mifflin,
1996.

Riso, Don Richard, *The Power of the Enneagram:
A New Technology of Self-Discovery*,
Simon & Schuster Audio, a Nightingale
Conant production, 1995. (2 cassettes)

Riso, Don Richard, with Hudson, Russ,
*Enneagram Transformations: Releases and
Affirmations for Healing Your Personality
Type*, Houghton Mifflin, 1993.

<u>Notes</u>

<u>Notes</u>